Foreword by
Dr. C. Thomas Anderson

not until he *left*

Dionne Arceneaux

Destiny Ink.

FIRST EDITION

Destinyink LLC
www.destinyink.org

ISBN 1-58588-176-7

Not Until He Left

Printed in Canada

Cover Design by Holly Sitzler
Cover Photos by William H. Caple III

Dedication

To my mother, Julia, for allowing me to share her story within my own. Thank God for Jesus and for healing us both.

To my spiritual parents, my mom and dad, Pastors Tom and Maureen Anderson, thank you for raising me, for loving me, and for seeing me through the blood of Jesus.

To my children, my gifts from the Almighty, I pray that you enjoy the richness of God's precious anointing and always know the benefits of fellowshipping and walking with Him daily. For this journey you two have taken with me, I pray that God's grace would cover every step we've taken together. I pray you two find your spirit-mates the first time and stay together till death do you part.

And finally for myself, for all that I am, in my frailty as well as my faith; I offer my life to God to do with as He pleases.

Table of Contents

Foreword

I count it an honor to write a foreword for this (Book). I hesitate to use the word book because it is more than a book. It's an experience, one that I believe many will find a rewarding, fulfilling and developmental experience. It has had a serious impact on my life to read it. Perhaps foreword is also a wrong word. Perhaps afterword would be more appropriate.

Dionne came to Living Word a strong, skeptical person on the exterior, but a fragile little girl on the inside. As you read through this experience, you will discover what the power of the Word of God has on an open heart. Dionne has always held a special place in my wife's and my heart and I believe she gives us way too much credit for the influence in her life and not enough credit to her commitment, perseverance and dedication to overcome, to grow and rise above her past and press on into the wonderful present life and future that God has planned for her.

—Dr. C. Thomas Anderson

Preface

Any Christian would agree that according to the Bible, God hates divorce. Most people who have been through a divorce will tell you they hate divorce, even if that divorce was necessary for their continued survival. Many of those will tell you that had there been another possible solution, they would have taken it, gladly.

Any reasonable person who has been through a divorce with children will tell you the children pay a higher price than the divorcing spouses. The scars they take with them oftentimes follow them into adulthood and into their own marriages where they recreate the cycle of divorce for the next generation. Many post-divorce children have problems in school socializing with others, establishing friendships, respecting authority, or they act out through negative behavior. This is not to say that two-parent homes don't go through some of the same challenges; I am saying that a divorce amplifies these issues even more, because what should be a team effort becomes a solo act or a one woman show.

No woman should be held captive within the confines of an abusive, destructive marriage while life is being choked out of her with the chords of religiosity that demand she remain captive. Many women wear their divorces on their sleeve or like an "S" on their chest, marking their "sin". It is not a sin to get a divorce. Sometimes it is more of a sin not to get a divorce, especially, if it is the only answer to a wrong question. While divorce is not the best answer, it is unfortunately too many times the only answer.

Within the first two years into my marriage, my husband had his first affair and after nine years, it ended much the same way it began—amid deception, conceit, and an above-accountability, laissez-faire attitude. Aside from his first affair, there was little remorse for the others. With every affair, a callous was created on his heart, his defiance grew stronger, his rebellion more blatant than the time before.

I am not writing this book to defame the character of my ex-husband. Part of me will always love him because he gave me two beautiful children. Part of me will always credit him as the catalyst to me rededicating my life to God. I continue to hope against all hope that grace and mercy extend to him long enough to not only hear the voice of God, but to heed that voice and fulfill his destiny.

I am writing this book to remove the excuse that so many divorced women use to remain victims—"I can't". I can't go back to school; I can't raise my children alone; I can't be successful; I can't be used of God. Not only can you, but God can use you to be a beacon of light to others. I do not want to be the new poster-girl for every woman looking for an excuse to get out of her marriage. But when you have stood, fasted, prayed, cried, not eaten, not slept, trying to figure out how to make it work, how to make it last, wondering what could have possibly gone wrong—then I am the sista' holding your hand, telling you I've been there and it's gonna be okay. You can get through this!

Over the last seven years God has taken my life and exploded it. In the last three years, I went back to school and completed my Associates and Bachelors Degrees. I plan to continue my education with graduate school, as well as my Doctorate Degree in Ministry. In the last two years, I purchased my first home and purchased my first car (from a dealer). In 2005 I was ordained and licensed as a pastor at Living Word Bible Church (LWBC), the largest faith-based church in the Phoenix-Metro area. I also work there full time as the Human Resources and Facilities Manager. I am the mother of two children who love God, know no lack, can pray for themselves and know how to intercede for others.

Still not convinced? During my marriage and several separations from my husband I was on DES, WIC, and TANF—all government-subsidized assistance programs for economically disadvantaged families. We have been evicted from an apartment, as well as a house. I have been without a car, money, or food. But if you want to know how God brought me out of Egypt, through the desert and into the Promised Land, don't put this book down. Read it and see for yourself what faith, submission, and obedience can really do.

I once read that God doesn't call the qualified, He qualifies the called. I am living proof of that very statement!

I didn't know how much
perseverance I had;

I didn't know how much
strength I had;

I didn't know how much
love I had;

I didn't know how much
faith I had—

Not Until He Left.

Introduction

What happens when you kiss a frog? For generations many fairytales have delighted us with the notion that when you kiss a frog it will morph into a handsome prince. I love those stories; I grew up with those stories. Many of us are fortunate enough to learn at an early age that this notion is limited to the boundaries of the fantasy realm. The rest of us learn the lesson after our lips are chapped and raw from kissing frog after frog after frog.

In my thirty-eight years of life and more than thirteen years in ministry I have met very few women who knew what it meant to be married. What is the role of the husband? What is the role of the wife as the helpmate? On its best or worst day, marriage takes skill. It is learned, not intuitive. This skill allows us to bask in the sunshine of the good days, as well as to navigate through the storms. It is a skill that is not successfully being taught in the secular and only now being taught in the Christian world. Unfortunately the divorce rate in both is about the same.

A man and a wife are supposed to be an outward reflection of the relationship between Jesus and the church. Jesus cares for her, protects her, loves her. He gave His life for her. She (the church) responds to His covering with honor, respect, adoration, affection, exalting words, and a harvest of love. When divorce happens, it breaks—no, it shatters that picture. God hates divorce because it breaks that picture, because it breaks relationship and fellowship. I know firsthand how divorce detours destiny, alters vision.

If God, the Creator, determined the value of marriage, then who are we to devalue it by reestablishing its value to fit our own desires, wants or "dis"wants. When my 1971 husband didn't want his 1968 model wife, and he traded it in on a newer, 1976 model, what he didn't realize was that a newer model, when driven by the same untrained, unskilled driver that was driving the 1968 model, would still have the same problems. It is not the vehicle; it is the driver. When we determine the value of marriage instead of He who cre-

ated it, we experience our present state of being—the devaluation of the marriage and the
breakdown of the marriage union.

God gave me a beautiful understanding
about the concept of marriage. It is the reason why I have resolved myself to not marry
again until I feel it settled in every fiber of
my being that my marriage will bring glory to
God. After being married and divorced from
my previous husband twice and now being
married only to Jesus, in hindsight, there
were many things my husband and I did to
ourselves and to each other that did not glo-
rify God in our lives and ultimately in our
marriage.

Throughout the first two sections of
this book, I will refer to my (now) former
husband as my husband, so as not to go back
and forth between married or divorced and
so you will always know to whom I am referring. For the third section of the book, I will
refer to him as my F. H. (former husband).
I am not printing his name in this book because the story and what God has taught
me through this is more important than the
names of the individuals. The facts of this
story are relevant only in reference to the

awesome power of God to take a broken life, redeem it and rebuild it.

The circumstance of my divorce from my husband for the second time in 2004 forced me to look back and see realistically what had brought me to this point. There were many choices I felt my husband made that were wrong, but since I can only be accountable for myself, I could only look at and into myself. Looking back, I knew there had been choices I made that were wrong and destructive to me personally and maritally. But nowhere in my life plan did I ever aspire to be a single mother of two, with limited education, and in great debt.

The second time we married, I thought it was our chance to prove everyone wrong and prove God right—we WERE meant to be together. I felt that God had put us together and I knew I had become the wife God called me to be, so what happened?

The fact is that even when God puts a man and a woman together, there is no fairy dust that keeps them together. It takes real, doubtless trust and unconditional love—you know, the love that goes past the tingle in your stomach on your first kiss; it's that "till death do us part" kind of love. It takes putting the other person's needs ahead of your own. It takes willing sacrifice and compromise—the option of divorce needs to be forever removed from the marital equation. You stay, you pray, you work it out.

As a couple, my husband and I failed to do that. To pray for him to stay when his heart and his belongings were already gone, would have been praying against his will. If God wouldn't violate his will and force him to stay, neither could I. Trust me, I tried everything to get him to come back—more sex, no rules of behavior, no requirement of respect from him towards me. He could come and go as he pleased—and he would, sometimes for days at a time. I even offered to work two jobs and suggested he stay home with the kids full time. It seemed reasonable at the time since I had worked two jobs for several years of our marriage. In the years that we were together, we experienced and caused each other enough hurt to last a lifetime.

I pray this book serves as a preventative tool for some, a restorative tool to others and a get-out-of-prison-free-card—if needed. When God issued a mandate for me to write this book, although sorely apprehensive, I became pregnant with it and could not stop until it was done. There will be no true rest for me until I give birth to this book.

The
Tragedy

A Flawed Blueprint

In 1999, God began to take me on a journey through my past to look at some ideals and foundational misperceptions that had become the cornerstone to my thinking, both about myself and about relationships. By 2003, while separated from my husband, I had come to terms with some harsh realities and took a long hard look at my life

Many changes had been made, some changes still in process. I no longer had the luxury of blaming anyone else for where my life was at the time. As my relationship with God was deepening, the layers of dysfunction, rejection, abuse, and hurt were slowly being removed layer by layer. The blueprint by which I had built my life and framed a marriage was terribly flawed.

I grew up in West Monroe, Louisiana on Ridge Drive with my great-great-aunt and great-great-uncle (Coach and Sista'). My grandmother's house was directly across the street. The women of Ridge Drive, when I was growing up, were very, very strong, dominant, forceful women. The men have been (historically) taken care of, instead of being cared for by their helpmates. The women paid the bills, worked full time, were well-educated, professional women and the men were around to facilitate things as delegated to them by their wives. They went to work when they were told to, they went to church when they were told to, they ate when they were told to and so on.

A perception was built in me that the women ran things and the men followed direction. Since we never talked about the dynamics of marriage and how to be successful at it—I deduced that being independent, strong, and in charge would make me more valuable to a future potential spouse. I was sorely mistaken. As I look back, I think my biggest problem was that I wanted to emulate the roles I saw and grew up with.

What I didn't know was that my grandfather had left my grandmother in horrific debt almost twenty years before I was born. Her strength and independence did not come from desire, but out of necessity. My grandmother wanted a man to be the head of the house. She wanted her man to be the man. Unfortunately (for me) we had that conversation a few decades too late.

My great-great-aunt, Sista', derived her strength from being in the professional realm in rural Louisiana in the 40s, 50s and 60s. She was a well-educated, Christian, professional educator. My childhood was filled with stories of how she and her colleagues fought for educational equality, voting rights, civil rights, and rubbed shoulders with the civil rights giants of the day. Being suc-

> A perception was build in me that the women ran things and the men follwed direction.

cessful in the professional arena demanded that she be smarter, stronger, and harder than her male (mostly white) counterparts. She just didn't know how to turn that switch off when she came home. Her strength was actually the key to her survival in the South. But it was not tempered with any kind of gentleness for those she loved. She loved on her terms.

I learned later that my great-great-aunt and my grandmother had both been married twice each. My mother, at the time of this book, had been marred three times and is currently single. Not to mention my own marital hopscotch—I think there's a spiritual implication there. Hmmm.

My great-great-uncle, Coach, the only man around the house when I was growing up, loved my great-great-aunt. He never tried to change her, but learned to embrace her strength. I theorize that he liked it because she took care of everything and he allowed it.

He went back to college and got his degree because she arranged it. He worked as a football coach, which he loved, and later as a principal, a career move planned by my great-great-aunt. I don't know what he did when living with my great-great-aunt became difficult. Whether they talked about it or he went outside of the marriage for comfort will remain forever unanswered.

I had one other uncle, my mother's brother, a classic, old school playa'. He was in the military and served our country in the Vietnam War. Once he got out of the military he lived out of state for many years when I was growing up. When he moved back to Louisiana, he worked for a large railroad company.

He was all fun, the life of the party. He went from relationship to relationship. Women loved his charm and his charisma.

When I was in college in the late 80s, he would make the three-hour drive to come pick me up and take me home for the weekends. We'd spend most of the drive home getting high. He and his boys had the best clothes, the best women and the best of lawless times. He knew God all his life. They just weren't close until towards the end of his life.

Then there was my biological father. His name isn't even on my birth certificate, but both his family and my family agree that he is my father. I met him when I was about eleven or twelve years old. I saw him again at my high school graduation. Then I saw him from time to time throughout my adult life. From what I heard about him, he was kind-hearted, fun, lovable, and very playful.

For him, none of these ingredients became the cornerstone to any marriage. He was a serial monogamist, going from one committed relationship to another. He was married once, very briefly, but this marriage produced no children, although four other women in his life would. I am the oldest and I have met two of my half-siblings and I know of one other whom I have not met. I know he loved all of our mothers and he loved all of us.

I have never questioned my father's love for me. He loved me as best he could. He was one of twins. His sister still lives in Louisiana and we talk often. He also had two brothers born within months of each other, each with a different mother and each bearing the same name as him. Many factors came together to make him the man he became. I will never judge him for his choices. They were his to make.

My limited memories of him include him telling me, whenever we talked, that he loved me. He would always ask me if I knew why he loved me. I would always answer, "I don't know." His response would always be, "Just because I do, baby girl." That memory, along with taking me out to hustle pool and him smoking that "oooweee", are what I remember about him the most.

I wasn't around him growing up, so there is a whole other side of me that I barely know. So many character traits of his I think I have, but I just don't know for sure. I do not know how he felt about marriage, commitment, God, and other perplexing life questions I would have loved to discuss with him. I will never be able to. I didn't even know his favorite color or favorite food. I knew so little about him. He represents little more than missing pieces in the puzzle of my life.

The reason I grew up in West Monroe, Louisiana was

> I have never questioned my father's love for me. He loved me as best he could.

because my mother moved to California when I was young and the family (my grandmother and her aunt and uncle) wanted me to stay in Louisiana with them and my mother consented. When my great-great-aunt and great-great-uncle got custody of me, I was about five years old. They were more than fifty years old.

I know now that the decision to leave me behind is one of the many decisions my mother wishes she could go back and change. She gave me the opportunity to have an amazing life, knowing no material lack. She made the best decision she could at the time with the resources and information she had. California was a new frontier to her and my father was coming in and out of her life. She was still trying to figure out where her own life was going and she didn't want her choices to have a negative impact on me. She would not know until decades later, how her choices would affect me and an unforeseen generation to come.

ATTENTION PARENTS—let me help you. Every choice you make ripples into the lives of your children. ATTENTION CHILDREN—let me help you. Every choice you make ripples into the lives of your family. This humanity journey has an undeniable, inescapable aspect of interdependence. Our choices do affect others, whether we like it or not.

A Child's Reflection

So many good and bad images flood my mind from growing up. As I said, I grew up in West Monroe, Louisiana with a lot of privileges. I had my own room for as far back as I can remember. I had my own television set, phone, and computer. I remember my family being very active in church, including choir rehearsal (twice a week), teacher's meeting, mission board meeting, Baptist Training Union, 10th District Association. I was President of Girl's Town in the mid 80s at the annual Louisiana Baptist State Convention Youth Encampment as well as President of the 10th District Youth Association. I grew up in a cultured environment, filled with classical music, theatre, fine dining and shopping, and the Black social elite.

Almost every area of my life insured my success, except two—sex and marriage. Sex was NEVER discussed! And I was surrounded by a few business marriages, not love story marriages. Whatever made marriage work was a secret no one had shared with me. Why sex was given to the union of marriage was something I did not hear until I was thirty years old. Marriage, in my mind, looked like a life sentence where I would be the guard and my spouse would be the inmate. I would get to decide meal times, job assignments, allowance, and hobbies.

Since life does not come with erasable ink, what is written, what is done, leaves a lasting impression that even God cannot erase. But He can use your experiences and weave them into an awesome testimony. The challenge becomes taking a negative and allowing God to turn it into a positive before it destroys you. There is one story within this book that had a lasting effect. It took God nearly twenty-five years to make this negative a positive. He had to work through many people coming into my life and change my perception about men after surviving what you are about to read.

When I was about three or four years old, my mother, who was never married to my father, married my stepfather. He was a truck driver, making cross-country hauls. I remember living for a short time with my mother on the semi that he drove. My stepfather was very physically abusive to my mother and occasionally to me.

My mother became pregnant and I had already been sent to live with my great-great-aunt by the age of five. My grandmother knew only to a limited degree the abuse my mother was suffering at the hands of my stepfather. My grandmother wanted my mother to move back home to

> Marriage, in my mind, looked like a life sentence where I would be the guard and my spouse would be the inmate.

West Monroe and live with her. Even after my sister was born; my stepfather's abuse did not subside. My mother finally got up the courage to leave and returned home amid threats from my stepfather that if he couldn't have her, no one ever would.

In the late summer of 1973, shortly after my mom had left my stepfather and moved back home, my stepfather was back in town and waiting to confront my mother. While the family was over at my house, my mother, my baby sister and I went across the street to my grandmother's to get something my grandmother needed us to bring back to her. All I remember is walking into the house and my stepfather surprising my mother. He and my mother began to argue and he began hitting her.

Back in the 70s they had these large glass flower vases that looked hand blown and stood about three feet high off the floor. I remember my stepfather picking up the one that my grandmother had sitting on her living room floor next to the couch. As he picked it up, I remember my mother throwing my sister (not quite yet a toddler) across the room where she landed on the couch. My stepfather hit my mother with that glass vase and began beating her mercilessly, with what I believe to be all the rage in his soul. And there I was, frozen. I hadn't moved since the first blow. My stepfather was trying to beat my mother to death and it was all playing out like a horror movie right before my very eyes.

My mother began to yell and scream for me to get out and get help. I ran to my house and I remember my great-great-uncle getting his gun and everyone running over to the house to see about my mother. My stepfather had already fled by the time we got over there. My sister was on the couch crying, but looked unharmed.

The next image I have is that of my mother standing in my grandmother's bathroom, naked, bleeding, picking glass out of her hair, most of her teeth knocked out, her head bashed in and the police on the way. I stared at her until someone noticed that I was there and made me stop looking. But before I moved, I allowed that image to be forever burned into my memory. Later someone said that I had saved her life by getting help. I didn't feel much like a savior. I felt like a scared little girl who just watched her mother come within inches of her own life.

I decided that very day that I would never look like the woman I saw in the bathroom. When I grew up I would have control, because if I surrendered it, it could cost me my life. If I didn't have control, my man would either leave me or kill me. I had to be stronger than him, if not physically, then mentally, if not mentally, then perceptionally—so I would NEVER find myself in a bathroom naked, picking glass out of my hair. We rarely talk about that day. Even now we only mention it briefly, maybe in conversation with other women when we are sharing our experiences or ministering about what we've been through. Today my mother lives with indentions in her skull you can feel through her scalp and a partial in her mouth from the teeth that were knocked out. She lives with the scars and the memories of that day and I will carry that image to my grave.

They say that what doesn't kill you can only make you stronger. That day I became strong, too strong—hard on the outside, soft and vulnerable in the inside. I became encased in that strength. It would prove to be my greatest asset and the cause of my downfall. As I grew up, I had this illusion of invincibility, life on my terms. Let no one in too far and I would be safe. My own personal greatest threat was growing on my own family tree.

The Root of My Evil

Knowing what I saw as a young girl, you now know or can imagine that I had no trust of men. My great-great-uncle was the only exception to that rule. He loved me dearly, purely, and I loved him. His solution to my experiences as a child was to protect me and shield me from as much of the world as possible; my life became very sheltered. I was not allowed to have any boyfriends or even talk on the phone to a boy. The only boys I saw were at church. My great-great-uncle made sure that I was untouchable. I was NEVER allowed to be alone in my home with a boy. I was not allowed to date without a chaperone until I had been presented to formal social society as a debutante at age seventeen.

I had my first boyfriend when I was in high school, in ninth grade, but could not go out with him until years later. Even though we were dating, we hardly ever saw each other, except at Carroll High School football games my great-great-uncle took me to. In tenth grade I saw him from time to time at school dances or when my family went to his family's restaurant. We didn't even have our first kiss until the summer of my fifteenth birthday.

Everyone in my home town expected us to get married some day. His mother was crazy about me and to this day has a picture of him and me from high school hanging in her bedroom in her house in Monroe. I remember him always treating me with kindness and gentleness. He even put up with every rule and boundary my great-great-aunt and uncle could come up with in order to see me.

No one had ever talked to me about men, relationships, sex, and all that. I found out about my menstrual cycle from my god-sister and a boxed kit for girls filled with pamphlets about my body and products I had never even heard of, let alone seen. My mother sent me the box from California when I was thirteen years old and my great-great-aunt sent me to my room to read through it and try out the products. To my great-great-aunt and uncle, all of this stuff was far removed from their life way before I came on the scene. My first period was not a celebration of my first step towards the journey into womanhood; it was more like a biological burden that came with their custody of me.

> No one had ever talked to me about men, relationships, sex, and all that.

Unknown to my first boyfriend, there was another relationship competing with ours. My first boyfriend was my first love, in the purest sense of the word. I did not have to protect myself from him or fight him off of me. He protected me and loved me. But there would be another I should have been protected from. All of the safeguards my family put in place to protect me from the world would only serve to seal me in with a predator. My shell was hiding a naïve, scared little girl with a deep dark secret. From the age of thirteen to the age of eighteen I would be seduced into a sexual relationship with a distant relative (a fourth cousin).

Even now it is hard to term it abuse. You may ask why. It is because this relative convinced me that our relationship was his way of protecting me from everyone else. When the relationship started, I didn't know what was happening to me or how to process it all. I believed everything my relative said to me. Up until that point, no one had ever said anything like the things he was telling me. Besides I trusted him. I believed everything that came out of his mouth. My time with him seemed secluded from the rest of the world. For the first time in my life, a very young life when this relationship was conceived, I felt pretty, special, wanted and loved, but the source of these feelings was not light. It was darkness; it was dysfunction.

My relative comes along who tells me he loves me, how important I am to him and how he wants to help me discover how beautiful I really am. This same man tells me how unique our love is and how it will never be shared with anyone else other than us. He said if he didn't love me and protect me, no one else would, that only he could truly show me how much he loved me and the "right" way to love and be loved, how this gift from him was only for me and no one else. It was an ugly, deceitful, life-altering secret.

My father had abandoned me. My stepfather had rejected me and wanted my mother dead. My identity was left to the determination of another person rather than my Creator—I never learned to look to Him to give me my identity, never knew I could. I had become wrapped up in how I performed, as a student or as a church youth leader, now as a young lover. When I wasn't performing, my life had no meaning. I had no worth. I was always looking for validation from someone, anyone. It made it easy for my identity to be misshapen by someone else.

I had a romantic sense of what love meant. This romanticism was derived from the music I listened to, the movies I watched and magazines I read. I wanted that life for my life and this is what I thought I had with him. This was a person I could be with for the rest of my life. This was a person who gave me value, who treated me like the most important thing in his life.

The small part of me screaming that this was wrong was overshadowed by my desire for love and acceptance. Every time I wanted to share our love with the family, I was warned that they would not understand it or appreciate it. He told me that what made it special was the fact that it was just between us. I even wanted to tell my first boyfriend, but by the time I had the courage to tell him, we were no longer dating. I was too scared to confide in anyone else.

It wasn't until I left and went to college almost five years after our relationship began that I learned that relationships like this were not normal. I had moved to a different part of Louisiana, about three hours from my hometown of West Monroe to Lafayette, Louisiana. I shared my experience with one childhood girlfriend, who was from my hometown, and as it turned out, she had gone through a similar experience. Now I felt ugly, ashamed, and stupid.

Amidst all of that, I never wanted this person to be taken out of my life. He was all I knew, all I had—the one person who I thought loved me. I would carry that guilt for the next decade. This book will be the first time many of my friends and most of my family have ever heard anything about it. I took that abuse and turned it into promiscuity, death-defying substance experimentation and utter ungodliness. I led a double life. In my late teens and early twenties, I did everything in my power to destroy my life with lawless, dysfunctional, self-destructive behavior which would continue for many, many years.

> In my late teens and early twenties, I did everything in my power to destroy my life.

I was frantically looking for answers, for some relief from my life, and I would come up empty every time. God was there whispering to me through old friends from the church camp I used to attend. He was trying to get my attention, but I was determined to live my life on my own (pitiful) terms without God, who in my mind had not been there for me before, so I was gonna show Him and do it by myself.

I honestly do not know what I was thinking. Everything I tried without God wasn't working, yet I refused to go back to God, repent and start over. God spared my life over and over, giving me chance after chance, and I was squandering every one of them. It would not be until several years later that I quit fighting against what God had placed in me, embraced it and chose to live for Him. I would have many more hard knocks before coming to that realization.

In 1989, I even married my best friend at the time, to avoid going back home or being forced to move to California with my mother after all my antics caused me to flunk out of college. I married him thinking he could fill the void I was filling with drugs. I did what I knew—the warden and the inmate. I made his life a living hell for about eighteen months.

To hear him tell it, it was nine months of bliss and nine months of hell. He served in Desert Storm as a marine. When he returned home from the military, he told me that the military was the most important thing in his life. He said following orders was the only way to survive, even if it meant doing things that would seem questionable stateside. He talked about all the ways he had been trained to kill people.

Well, that was all I needed to disconnect. With his training and military background, I thought my days were numbered. In one of the fights we had, he had punched

through a wall right past my head. In another fight he hugged me until I almost
passed out.

The day I left him, he was expecting
to come home from work and talk about our
future. He had only been home from Desert
Storm for a short time. He wanted to stop
all the fighting and work things out. I went
into survivor mode and created in my mind
that this was just the kind of story he would
give me right before killing me. I convinced
him that when he arrived home that night
we would sit down and talk and figure some
things out.

When he went to work that morning,
I sold most of the furniture in our apartment, emptied the house of all that belonged
to me, packed up my car and left. He came
home to an empty house and a missing wife
and no answers, not so much as a letter or
note. This is not the husband that this book
is about. This is the husband I should have
never had—he would have been, and is now,
much better off as my friend.

An Unsettled Soul

Right before I moved to California in 1992, I met my husband (the one the book is about). He was three years younger than me. I was working in a retail clothing store during the day and was managing a gentleman's club (you are gasping right now, I'm sure) in Lafayette on weekends.

When he and I met, he was not even old enough to go into the bar where I worked, nor did he want to. I was the first person to get him high on marijuana and later cocaine. He was responsible for getting me to quit working clubs and start going back to church. I had moved to California in January of 1992 and he convinced me to move to Arizona the following May for a chance at a better life in a different city where I could start over. It also gave me a reason to move away from the relative I had the affair with as a teen. After our relationship ended, we did not see each other very much.

My then boyfriend (later husband, the one the book is about) required that we attend church and be faithful tithers. He was surprised at my knowledge of the Word. I must admit, so was I. He was further surprised at how involved I was in church as a child. He was even more surprised when I took him to one of the Baptist Youth Camps where I had been a leader and served as President as a teenager. He had a chance to meet some of the people who knew a different Dionne, the one that used to love God and live for God, who grew into the woman who avoided God, didn't trust Him or the men He created.

My husband and I dated for two years and were married in August of 1994 in Mesa, Arizona. My husband was my prince charming. He could tell me the sky was pink and I changed my reality of an obviously blue sky to an imagined pink one. He would weave these incredible stories of wealth and growing up with privilege, as I did. He told me his father owned property in Louisiana and owned oil wells. He told me his best friend in Arizona had a plane we could travel on, and other fantastic stories.

He knew some things about my past, but he never knew about my past relationship with my relative. In the few times we had all seen each another, my husband would always say that there was some-thing not right about him and something very strange about our relationship. I always dispelled it

> I really thought this person (this man) would make my life all better.

by telling him we had been close since childhood and it was nothing to be concerned about.

My husband promised to always be there for me, to protect me—to take me away from all of the hurt and pain I had suffered growing up. I really thought this person (this man) would make my life all better. The life questions I so desperately needed answers to, I thought I would find in him. He was quiet, rather reserved, not argumentative. He let me behave as good or as bad as I wanted to. We prayed together, served in church togeth-er, sought God together—it was a dream come true, with just an occasional nightmare.

I was a very controlling and domineer-ing wife. I thought I had to be in order to protect myself and my life. I trusted my husband as much as I could. Life had already taught that if I wasn't in control, it could mean my life. If I wasn't in control, then someone would take advantage of me. It was just a matter of time. This mindset drove me to be my own self-fulfilling prophet. The things I feared most, I brought upon myself through fear and suspicion.

Running alongside my issues, my husband struggled to find peace of his own. His upbringing was riddled with infidelity, multiple marriages and divorce—same as mine. He was battling generational curses of his own and a stronghold of a lustful and unquenchable heart. Less than two years into our marriage, my husband confessed to his first affair (Woman #1). At the time, we were sharing a large condo with my mother who was estranged from her third husband. Although the knowledge of the affair was devastating, I faced it very analytically. I figured that since I had so much baggage and junk, some of which he still didn't know, then who was I to judge and condemn. If we could get past this, we could survive anything.

After his confession we stayed together and tried to work through it, as hard as it was.

I became distant and cold, both physically and emotionally unavailable. I was reminded of past hurts and betrayals that he was still unaware of. I became mean and difficult to live with. I became suspicious of his comings and goings. Our marriage had truly become the warden and the prisoner relationship I had inadvertently prophesied over my own life years earlier.

Our first child, Rionne, was born in 1996. In the fourth month of my pregnancy, I contracted Toxemia (preeclampsia) and went into the hospital. I was admitted in the fifth month of my pregnancy and was supposed to remain hospitalized for the rest of my pregnancy. Two months later, twenty-six weeks into my pregnancy, I gave birth to our daughter. She was born three months premature, weighing only 1.8 pounds. Our lives became consumed with her and her well-being. She stayed in the hospital for what would have been my last trimester.

One of our first outings as a family was to attend our church on Father's Day, June 13, 1996. My husband wept as he talked from the pulpit about how our daughter's birth had changed him as a man. How he

would always be there for her and for our
family. How glad he was that God had created him as a man and called him to be the
head of his household and protector of his
beautiful daughter. There was not a dry eye
in our church that day.

I became a stay-at-home mom, to care
for Rionne, and my husband worked very
hard to provide a life for us. We were active together in church and in church leadership, yet his heart remained unquenched
in its search for fulfillment. Over the next
couple of years, there would be five more affairs—that I would know of.

In the spring of 1998, my relatives came
into town. The relative that I had the relationship with as a teenager was with them.
We began to talk about our previous relationship, and I began to tell him how I wanted
to tell my husband and how I hated what I
had done and how what happened between
us made me feel. I told him how it had taken
me years to realize that my love for him was
wrong and ungodly. He tried to explain to me
that he truly loved me and could not help his
feelings and he didn't think that they were
wrong, just wrongly timed. He tried to tell

me of the dysfunction he grew up with and how his father had a long standing mistress and addiction to pornography that had been the framework of his belief system. To my amazement, I realized that in his mind, his love for me was true.

As we sat there talking, he began to rub my shoulder and I just froze. I do not know if I felt thirteen again or if I was in shock, but I could not move. As he touched me, I felt like I was not even there, but that I was watching a man take advantage of a little girl and I was a spectator of a very bad dream. My heart and my mind were screaming out—but

Over the next couple of years, there would be five more affairs— that I would know of.

no one was hearing me. I was not making a sound. I was glad to hear my husband driving up into the driveway. I didn't sleep that entire night and I remember every time I would doze off, I flinched, reliving the events of earlier that evening.

During this same time my mother and her current husband were going through their own struggles. Her husband had a drug abuse problem. He would steal from my mother and go on drug and alcohol binges where he wouldn't come home. If he did come home, he wouldn't talk to anybody. He was a recluse who rarely interacted with the rest of us.

As my husband's affairs continued, I recall one young lady coming to our house and presenting herself pregnant, claiming that the unborn child was my husband's (Woman #2). During this time period my husband spent little time at home. The young lady my husband had this affair with kept coming to our house, trying to talk to my him. He claimed that she was pregnant from a married man she had been seeing in California. My husband said he met her at her job at a local convenience store and was trying to help her get to California because he felt sorry for her. She gave birth to her daughter in January of 1999, according to more recent court documents, my husband's daughter. Our second child, a boy, would be born six months later.

Confession is Good for the Soul—Not

With all the chaos of my mother's deteriorating marriage and our constant arguments, my husband decided that we should move out and get our own place. In late 1998, we moved into our own apartment. I was three months pregnant when we moved. A few months later my husband became involved with a young lady, not the pregnant woman who came to our old house, but another young lady (Woman #3), that he would later move in with while we were still married and I was almost seven months pregnant with our second child. He lived between her apartment and ours. To make matters worse, our apartment was downstairs and hers was upstairs on opposite sides of the same apartment unit in a very large apartment complex.

One of the statements my husband had made to me was that maybe we just didn't belong together because our backgrounds were so different. He also said that he had

made so many mistakes and had so many affairs, he didn't understand what was wrong
with him and that he just wasn't good for
me. He could never expect me to want to
work things out. He said he felt like our
marriage was a mistake.

Just before I was due to deliver our son
and after months of my husband telling me
that he couldn't love me and didn't want to
be with me, I decided that if I were to tell
him what had happened to me as a teenager
he would realize that I wasn't perfect either.
He would now be able to understand why
I was the way I was, why I had chosen so
many methods of escape. He could forgive
me, I could forgive him, we could move on
and have a fairytale life.

When I played this out in my mind, it
had a happy ending. It was a romantic scene
drawn on a mental imaginary canvas. It
turned out to be the worst mistake of my life.
My husband called me some of the most ungodly names I have ever heard or been called
since. He blamed me for the abuse and the relationship with my fourth cousin. He blamed
me for never speaking out or getting help, and
for not telling him sooner so he could, as he put

it, "kick his —." According to him, both his problems and our marital problems were all my fault. I was the worst thing that had ever happened to him. What I had done was unforgivable. In his eyes, I became filthy that day and have remained so from that day to this one.

He even went so far as to say that maybe our son really wasn't his. I

> When I played this out in my mind, it had a happy ending. It was a romantic scene.

explained to him that nothing had happened since I was a young girl, that nothing had happened on the night he was referring to. I tried to tell him that I had never had an affair in the five years we'd been married. But by now he was on a roll and wouldn't hear anything other than his own voice cursing and shouting at me. He claimed that I was the cause of his sin and his need to go outside of our marriage for happiness.

All my demons had caught up with me and were residing in my soul, tormenting me. I felt alone, more alone that any human being should ever feel. During the day, I would work because I had to. I worked when I could convince myself to leave the house. I didn't talk much to my co-workers or to my family. My daughter and my unborn son became the only two reasons I got up day after day. At night, I would cry until my eyes were puffy and almost swollen shut.

My husband and his current girlfriend (Woman #3) had to pass in front of our apartment to get to the mail or to get to her car to leave our apartment complex. For weeks I found myself sitting by the window, looking through the window blinds, watching them through the sights of a gun my husband had bought me years earlier for my protection. I tried to contemplate the consequences of that decision and weigh it against the relief I would feel if I just killed him and ended this slow agonizing pain.

On May 4, 1999, I went into labor at work and one of my co-workers called my husband. I really did not want him to be there at our son's (Roman) birth. Going through the last trimester of my pregnancy alone was only complicated by having him at our son's birth knowing that he was going back to the apartment he shared with his girlfriend. In the hospital he teased me relentlessly about the fairness of our son's skin and how he looked nothing like my husband's side of the family. I brought my son home and was left alone to care for myself, a newborn, and a three-year-old toddler. An unforgettable statement my husband made to me was to let him know if "his" daughter needed anything, but that me and my ~!@#$ son were on our own.

My depression would come in waves. Some days I was fine. Then there were days when I hid in my house, shut the blinds and pretended not to be at home. At night, I would cry until I dry heaved and could hardly catch my breath. Having my two children was my only connection to sanity. Now I was home during the day and the reality of where life had brought me was overwhelming.

I even contemplated taking my own life, and if the following story did not sound so pathetic, it would be laughable. As my depression worsened, the thought of suicide became a pacifier that would fill my mind for hours at a time. But I did not want my kids to grow up with the stigma of a mother who had committed suicide, so that dictated that I would have to kill them first and then take my own life. Then I didn't want my mom to live with that

stigma either, or have to live without her oldest daughter and her grandchildren, so I would
have to kill her as well. Somehow I would
have to get her to come over, kill her first, then
my children, and then me. Considering that
my mother had escaped death once, it seemed
wrong for her death to be at my hands. Then
if I did kill her first, would I have enough for-
titude left to kill my children or would I be too
overcome with grief from killing my mother
that I couldn't continue. Then I'd be going to
jail for killing my mother, but I would still be
alive. My mother would be dead, when she
wasn't even the initial intended victim—I was.
And to top it all off, with me being in jail for
murder, my husband would end up with custody of my children, including a son he didn't
want, nor believed was his. My children would
have to visit me in prison, that is, if their father
would allow it, and another woman would be
by his side raising my children as their mother
. . . like Madea says, "Hell to the Naw." This
psychosis went on and on and on. I was tired
from over-thinking it all, it just became foolish, so I gave up that plan.

At the end of that psychotic episode, I
remember starting to cry and not being able

to stop. My children were asleep and I was crying out to God, telling Him how He had let me down and how He must be out to get me. Looking back over my life, it was a disaster that He sat back and watched happen on His big screen. I told God I knew that He hated me. I was now a statistic, a single mother, with no job, limited education, no hope, no future, no help and a complete embarrassment to my family. Why did God hate me so?

> I told God I knew that He hated me. I was now a statistic.

In that dark night, one of the darkest nights in the thirty-one years of my life there was a small voice that spoke and asked me a question? When did someone else's opinion of you matter more than mine? I knew in my heart it was God and that night was the first time we had talked, I mean really talked, in many, many years. He reminded me of how I got Spirit-filled at the Baptist Youth Encampment, though I had never used my gift. If I can be real, my talk with God was very difficult. It was not just a friendly, get-reacquainted-with-God-chit-chat. I didn't believe what God was saying to me. In my heart, it all sounded vaguely familiar, like the voice of someone I had known from long ago, but hadn't heard from in a while.

I had gotten so far from God that He felt a million miles away. He promised to get me through that night; I promised Him nothing. I told Him that I didn't trust Him and that I couldn't love Him because I didn't trust Him. He only reminded me that He loved me no matter what, that His prayer for me was that one day I would love Him back, but that it was up to me. He said that He had been there all along, trying to talk to me, but I had turned a deaf ear. He reminded me of people scattered throughout my past, divinely sent by Him to be positive influencers in my life, and how I disregarded them. He said how much it hurt Him that someone had used their free will to violate mine, how He had saved my life on many occasions when I was determined to throw it away.

He challenged me to step out and try Him all over again. At first, I said no. I told Him too much had happened. My life was worthless, my future hopeless, my children destined to fall in the same traps that all of

us before them had fallen into. God promised
that this time would be different if I gave Him
my whole heart; if I surrendered my life to
Him, He would take it, recreate it, give it back
to me and make it better than I could ever
imagine. I told God that if I trusted Him and
He abandoned me, I would tell everyone that
He is a liar and had failed me. God promised
me that night, that is the one thing He could
not do. My answer to Him was, "We shall
see." He promised me everything; I promised
Him nothing, other than my weak, frail human threats. What a benevolent and loving
God to allow me such indulgences.

The
Triumph

A Real Living Word

After that night, I won't say that heaven opened and a blinding light came from the sky and all was right with my world— Uuaa, NO. The next morning God had to remind me of our conversation the night before. That night I prayed, not for Him to fix things or change things; I simply offered Him me. I had nothing else to give Him. I asked Him to teach me how to trust Him, how to love Him, how to love myself. I offered Him my children and prayed for Him to keep them in His care. I wanted to be little more than their caretaker. I needed God to be their father. I felt I had nothing to give them as a mother because I did not know how to be a mother.

I offered God a day, a whole day; that was as far as I could see. My sister-in-law (at the time) called me, saying that I needed to get child support for my children and assistance for myself. For the first time I would be seeking help living my life. I got on federal assis-

tance. I hated it, but needed it. After my husband was served with child support papers, he
decided to convert them to divorce papers.

During that time, two miracles happened. One, God gave me total peace about
my divorce. I didn't want it, but God told me
not to fight it and so I didn't. The other miracle was that a church I had gone to for alms
(free financial support given to individuals of
church congregations) and been denied, was
now calling me to apply for a job. The miracle
in this is I had not applied for a job, nor did I
attend this church—my mother did. My son
was about three or four weeks old. At my previous job I was one week short of a year and
therefore did not qualify for maternity leave
or any type of pay past my last day worked.
I had no income and no job. How did this
church even find me and want me to come in
for an interview?

I was attending a mid-size Baptist
church where my husband and I had served
in leadership together. I had only met Pastors
Tom and Maureen once and only visited their
church on special occasions and holidays. I remember dropping my mom off for service and
the pastor's wife walking up to me and ask-

ing me if I still worked at my church because
they were looking for an assistant. Then she
walked away and discontinued our conversation. I came back on another Sunday a week
or so later to pick my mom up from church
and the pastor's
wife walked up to
me again, asked me
a similar question,
then went on to say

During that time, two
miracles happened.

---

that I should really apply because when she
saw me, she prayed and felt the anointing and
felt that it should be me.

Frankly, I thought she was crazy. I in-
terviewed the following week under duress. I
was rude and callous to everyone but the pastors. I met with the Church Administrator,
but had to wait an additional week to meet
with the CFO. I remember complaining about
how the church was "begging" me to come
in and interview, I came in and then got put
off for a week—hurry up and wait, I thought.
This was still, in fact, the same church that
wouldn't even help me just a couple of weeks
earlier and now they wanted to give me a job.

When I met with the CFO, he said that
his interview was just a formality because his

family (he is the pastors' son, as is the Church Administrator) all liked me and wanted to hire me, but needed the approval of all four. I retorted sharply with, "What if I don't want a job here. I don't even know if I like ya'll." He responded with, "Well, we don't know if we like you either, so why don't we just try it for a month and see how it goes?" He asked me how much I was making at my last job. I told him. He offered to pay me $1.00 more an hour and I took the job.

So on July 7, 1999 with a seven-week-old baby and a three-year-old daughter, I started work as the Senior Pastor's Personal Manager. God had taken me from slave to sin to second in command of the senior pastor's life in one big step. My mind was spinning. It didn't make any sense and I couldn't explain it if I wanted to. I had no good reason why I was given this job and this opportunity. I brought with me my baggage, bad attitude, good work ethic and sharp wit. I had a high respect for spiritual authority (especially pastors) and a desire to get off assistance as quickly as I could. I didn't talk to my new co-workers very much, nor did I socialize with them or hardly anyone else at the church at all. I stayed to myself, too afraid to get close, still afraid of getting hurt.

The first thing the Andersons did for me was to provide me with transportation so I could get back and forth to work. They learned that I was sharing a car with my mother and the only other alternative was to ride the bus. I, Dionne Nichelle (Jones) Arceneaux, former club manager, party-goer, drug user, etc., was now working for the senior pastors of a very large, predominantly white, Word and Faith church. These people opened up every part of their lives to me. Frankly, they were freaking me out. I kept waiting for something to go wrong.

Shortly after being hired, I met with Dr. Anderson, the Senior Pastor. I wanted to tell him that I was going through a divorce, in case that would affect my employment—it never did. And I wanted my chance to bash my husband to someone other than my family. Dr. Anderson calmly told me that if I had treated him like I treated my husband, he would have left, too. He joked about my warden and inmate routine, asking me which one was I? He didn't looked surprised when I told him I played the role of warden.

Dr. Anderson went on to explain that my husband's choice to commit adultery was his choice and it could not be justified by my bad behavior. He explained how adultery is a life-changing choice, with lasting repercussions that begin with the potential loss of relationship and family. Not repenting of it and turning from it, but rather seeking to find a way to validate it, took away my ability to choose to stay or try to make it work. My choices were mine to own up to. My husband's choices were his. Neither of us could blame the other.

Dr. Anderson also cautioned me that I could only be accountable for me. He kept me focused on my responsibility to forgive but to learn healthy boundaries and raise my standards. Dr. Anderson told me I needed to press in to the Holy Spirit to begin to learn how to make wise choices and how to become the person God had always wanted me to be. He went on to explain that I was controlling and somewhat surly. He understood it as my defense mechanism against hurt. I didn't know how to open up to people, so I kept them far away or close through the same method—control and manipulation. He suggested that I be mentored by his wife.

And then he said something I will never forget. He said, "Dionne, You can trust us. We are just people. We love God and we love His people. We can love you into becoming the person God always wanted you to be."

> He was the first man to come into my life since my great-great-uncle that wanted nothing from me.

I acted all hard, like his words didn't affect me. But at that moment, God, through this man, had melted my heart. As I left his office, he said, "You'll just have to become one of our kids."

At that moment, his motive became clear. He was the first man to come into my life since my great-great-uncle that wanted nothing from me, but wanted me to have it all. There would be nothing that I could do for him, other than to love him as one of his own children. This man wanted to see me have a better life. My eyes opened a little wider that day. God had hired me to help me. I wasn't there for Living Word Bible Church. I was there because I needed to receive a living word—for myself. I needed Living Word Bible Church more that they needed me.

For the first time in my life, I knew without a shadow of a doubt that I was not being looked at as a commodity, liability, status quo requirement or affirmative action directive. I was finally being looked at as a human being—valuable, wanted, accepted and loved. The potential of my destiny had just caught up with and was now overcoming the disasters of my past.

Dionne, Behold Your Mother

I began to spend a lot of time with Dr. Anderson's wife, Pastor Maureen Anderson, more affectionately known as Pastor Mama. For weeks after I started working for them, she kept getting my name wrong. She called me everything from Donna, to Diane, to Diana, to Dana—anything other than Dionne (Dee Onn, like Leon, but with a "D").

One day I decided to call her out on it and I just said, "Why don't you just call me Dee?" She paused for a second and then quickly responded, "You know what I think? I think you have rejection, because I can't seem to remember your name and its not my fault." Then I really thought, this little woman is C R A Z Y for real. She then began to pray in the Spirit and said, "Yep, that's it." She continued and said, "But I can pray you free of that if you want me to."

By then there was nothing I could do, she already had my head in her hand and

was in full blown attack on the spirit of rejection and abandonment that had controlled
and dictated my life for so many years. In
that same moment, she said almost verbatim
what her husband had said just earlier that
month. "Well, I guess you'll just have to become one of our kids." Needless to say, she
has never forgotten my name since.

It is awesome for me to see how God
has made these people my people—my
church, my family. I laid down my former
life and picked up the life God intended for
me. I was now serving in this ministry lov-
ingly, loyally, and fully committed. Before, I
was only committed to Dionne. Nothing or
no one would stand in the way of my survival, even if they were only a perceived threat.
Now I was thinking about other people and
putting God first. Funny, huh!

My mother prayed for me to come
to Living Word Bible Church and become
a member almost six years before I came.
When I did come to visit LWBC, I made fun
of her, the church, and its people. My (biological) mother, Julia gave me the freedom to
be mentored and loved by Dr. Anderson and
Pastor Maureen as one of their children. She

gave me to them, to raise, to help me grow up (at thirty years old). Even as an adult, I had a lot to learn. If it weren't for my mother, I would not be here, in more ways than one.

Most of the abuse shared in this book, my mother only became recently aware of. I had carried many of these secrets in my heart and had vowed to myself to carry them to my grave. What God began to teach me was that these secrets gave others control over me. I ran from the exposure of these secrets and they pre-

> What God began to teach me was that these secrets gave others control over me.

vented me from being true to myself, true to God and true to others. It was not important to share all of this with everyone I met, but it was important for me to face it and get out from under the fear, intimidation, and shame that had come with it.

This way, at the very least, my tragedy will serve some good as it ministers to the needs of others. As I minister, I do not have to worry about my past catching up with me or someone trying to cause a scandal with the facts of my past. It is what it is—good and bad. It is my life's history, written in blood on stone pages, now covered in the blood of Jesus—forever. What the enemy tried to use to destroy me, God has used as a cornerstone and stairway to an awesome destiny.

Not Choosing Life Marked Me For Death

As a child, there was this concept of right behavior that was placed in me, but this right behavior had no foundational definition. I was told repeatedly, "Don't let me catch you…" (you can fill in the blank with any number of phrases, such as "playing in the street," "talking to a boy," "stealing stuff out of stores.") I learned how to not get caught, but I was still doing wrong. What I did not have was the skills to make right choices because it was the right thing to do. As long as I didn't get caught, then whatever I was doing was technically right—at least at the moment. The voice of God within me was drowned out by the noise that had become my life.

When your mind can convince you that something morally wrong is right, you will believe it and then act it out. Let me explain it the way my dad, my spiritual dad, Dr. Anderson, explained it to me. When a child obeys from the heart, that child doesn't want to hurt the heart of his/her parents, and if the child is a Christian, he/she doesn't want to hurt the heart of God. There is a relationship cultivated between the child and the parents that is in the heart of the child to make right choices because those right choices are mutually beneficial to the relationship. Whereas a child who only obeys out of the soul (the mind, the will, and the emotions), which are subject to environment and whim, it doesn't make a proper cornerstone to right behavior and thinking. If the heart is disconnected, the child WILL do wrong; it is only a matter of time. Why? The heart is not connected. When the heart is not connected, there will be rebellion and sin. The gauge of right and wrong will be adjusted to fit the situation rather than being set to the truth. The soul obeys it, and the flesh carries it out because the spirit requires it to do so.

I never learned that sex is a gift to the marriage union, that sex is meant to be celebrated as a glorious part of the marriage. The marriage bed is undefiled. It is only "dirty" or sinful when it is used outside of the definition of He who created it. When I was growing up, sex was already in the dark, not honored, not talked about—then my behavior mirrored that belief. After suffering the sexual abuse that I did, promiscuity seemed reasonable since I always kept it quiet and hidden. Sex was never beautiful.

After I was seduced into giving up my very essence, I decided not to let anyone take it from me again or trick me out of it, but I would give it on my own manipulative terms. The thing that God had given me to give as a gift to my husband has been tainted, abused

> If the heart is disconnected, the child WILL do wrong; it is only a matter of time.

away and then perverted by the enemy into being misused by me to his glory, the glory of the devil. That was then, this is now.

One of my heart's desires is to minister to women who have endured such deception or abuse, to let you know that you are not alone. My other reason is that as God continues to use me for His glory, whatever I can do to build His kingdom is my honor and privilege. There are so many women who have made mistakes and are carrying the weight and shame of those choices around their necks, and it is choking the life out of them. That's not God! Let me help you. If God can use me, Sweetie, please believe, He can use you. Your disaster can indeed lead to your destiny. God can take the same steps that once were leading you straight to hell without Him as your stairway to heaven with Him.

There are also millions of women trapped in unhappy, torturous, abusive marriages. Hear me well, abuse is not dirty socks on the floor or your husband working a lot and being too tired to talk to you or take you out when he comes home. I am talking about real abuse—adultery, physical beating, rape, cursing and verbal attacks. A man who loves God, works hard, honors his wife, and cares for his children, if he were my husband, would be met at the door with a hot dinner, his slippers in hand, with me wearing little more than high heels and a gift wrap bow (ha ha ha ha).

God Can't Use Me, I've Done Too Much

When God brought me to LWBC and things actually started to go well for me, it was almost too much for me to handle. My past kept screaming at me how unworthy I was to be here and how if these people ever found out about my past they would turn their backs on me forever. I had run so far from God, the thought of Him wanting to use me was almost nauseating to me. I thought only good Christians could be used by God, that people who were used by God but who had made some bad choices had gotten their lives together way before they were my age. God, I've done too much! My voice chimed in and sang lead while the blues and trash choir sang back up in the "I've done too much" gospel suffering-for-the-Lord musical tribute. Surely God must have missed something on my rap sheet or maybe He had just made a mistake on my divine appointment to this church.

I used to give the staff, my new co-workers, tidbits of my past to see their reactions, but within a short period of time, I came to learn these people were real people. None of us was perfect (still aren't). Many of their lives were just as tattered and torn as mine. The common thread was their love for God, submission to the Holy Spirit and their commitment to building better lives—not just for themselves, but for others, too.

I remember confessing to Pastor Tom something from my past and immediately I felt, "Oh, this is it. I'm out this time for sure." When I called him and shared these experiences with him, he cried. The pastor of thousands of sheep cried over one (me). He was hurt for me and what I had gone through rather than going with the natural human inclination to cast judgment. He told me that day that I was important. Yes, I did good work and yes, he was happy to have me as an employee—but more important to him than my work was me and how this incident had affected me.

He went on to tell me that LWBC is not a magical place. It is simply a house of God built on prayer and obedience. He told

me that I could go on making one bad choice after another or I could hear the voice of God and commit myself to heeding it. Just like God had promised me a short time earlier, Pastor Tom told me that it wouldn't be easy, but it would be worth it. He said my life could have

> My life could have either the limits I set on it, or in Christ Jesus, I could have a life of endless possibilities.

either the limits I set on it, or in Christ Jesus, I could have a life of endless possibilities.

I got off the phone and wept, but these tears were different. Not since I was a little girl had a man shed pure tears for me. My great-great-uncle cried when he knew I had seen my mother beaten. He cried again when I graduated from high school, and the last time he cried was on his deathbed when he put my hand in my husband's hand and laid his hand on top of ours, giving us his bless-ing to be married. This man, my pastor, had become my dad in every connotation of the word. He was laying down his life for me and had loved me into safety and security. He and Pastor Maureen had carved a special place in my heart. Few times had I felt the tangible love of God. This was one of them.

It still amazes me how God can build and has built many lives and ministries out of building blocks that confuse the wisest of men. All God needed from me was the freedom to operate in my life; all He needed was my permission. My will had to line up with His. It is not bondage, but true freedom. I knew why this sense of freedom came with responsibility, because there are more choices to make when you are free in Christ than as a slave to sin. In sin, I had no choice. The flesh and the sinful nature were driving me like cattle to the slaughterhouse.

I have to stop here and offer Jesus to the reader of this book. If you are tired of being a slave to sin and you are ready to become royalty, why wait? Let's do it now. It is a simple yet profound and life changing choice. Yes, we all have the God-given-free-will right to choose to do wrong, but why? When you use your will to go against God's will and do wrong, you join the ranks of the living dead, absent of real joy, prosperity, favor and blessings, all of which are so readily available. The second most important decision of your life is who you will marry; the first is salvation. It is not a matter of finding God, trust me. He's not lost, but without Him, you are. Just turn around and tell Him, "Okay. I am done doing this life thing on my own because I keep messing it up; God let's try it Your way for a change."

> *Dear Father God, I believe that Jesus is the one true Son of God, that He was crucified to pay the price for sin and that He was raised from the dead so I may have everlasting life. Father God, I ask you to forgive me of all of my sins and I ask your son, Jesus, to come into my life, come into my heart, be my Lord and my Savior, in Jesus' name. I ask the Holy Spirit to guide me, protect me, and help me daily in my new walk with Him.*
> *Amen*

Welcome to your new life. If heaven didn't open and the glory cloud didn't hover, its okay—you made the choice and all of heaven was a witness. The first step has been made. Every day won't be perfect, but every day will be a God-given gift, complete with opportunities to do right or wrong. You now have something a large part of the world doesn't have, an Advocate, a Savior, a Helper, an up close and personal Jesus. Get a Bible. See what God has to say about you, life, love, and destiny. God is a God of relationships. Allowing God to show you why He created you delights Him. Find out, from the Creator what His intended design and purpose is for you. You are God's creation, bound only to His design, not the opinion of another created being. I know you may have been through a lot, or you are going through a lot. Take it one God-given day at a time.

Might I suggest a passage of scripture God used to begin to show me what He thought of me—Psalm 139. You'll be amazed at what God thinks about you. Oh, and find a church home, a good one. God will lead you so you are not swimming upstream alone.

Welcome to your journey of discovery—who you are in Christ and who Christ is in you.

Life 101

I had rededicated my life to God and was doing okay, but I still had a lot of work to do internally. I wasn't living in the total prosperity or peace that surpasses understanding, and I definitely didn't have unspeakable joy. In the scripture I mentioned earlier, Psalms 139, there is a verse that says, "I am fearfully and wonderfully made." I felt anything but fearfully or wonderfully made. I subscribed more to the accidentally and woefully made.

I think what I struggled with the most was the truth that God really did love me and had not forsaken me all those years. I had grown up feeling like little more than a surprise to my mother and a deniable burden to my father. I thought that somehow I had been born unnoticed by God. Somehow I had slipped out (so to speak) under the radar. Based on my past, I decided that God had no plan for me, and I had been left to fend for myself.

I had to go back to the basics. At thirty years old, I was learning how to go to God (my Creator) and get the created plan for my life. I had to learn how to hear from God and what His voice sounded like. I had to learn how to trust Him. I had plenty of little trials and challenges that gave me opportunities to do just that. Trusting God meant allowing Him to instruct me as to what needed to change within me, and then me letting Him remove those things from me.

I could clearly see, within a short time, that I was my own worst enemy. My words were very negative, my confessions sparse and pessimistic. I was bringing trouble to me rather than using the Word of God to raise a standard to stand against trouble. For example, I would talk about how hard my life was by myself and how I could never take care of two children on my own. And sure enough, I was barely taking care of the three of us and I hated being a single mom. I spoke failure instead of favor and then acted surprised when failure came. I had to learn how to capture my thoughts and renew my mind.

My first step was to read the Word of God in a different way. I did not read it all the way through from Genesis to Revelation, nor did I read it through on a one year plan. I allowed God to read it to me. I know it sounds strange, but I began to read the Bible as if God were reading it to me. I knew the areas I struggled with—joy, peace, prosperity, blessings, and favor. So I used Pastor Maureen's *Discovering the Power of Confession* book and began to meditate on

> I could clearly see, within a short time, that I was my own worst enemy.

the scriptures I fought against the most. Now, when I say fought against, I mean these are the biblical concepts that were hard for me to accept as true for myself. Even though I was reading the Word, it didn't always really seem real to me. It seemed like it was working for those around me, but not for me, at least not yet.

Slowly the Word began to come alive. The more I read and meditated, the more hungry and thirsty I became. I was excited about this new relationship, the depth of it, and the satisfaction that came with true intimacy with God. I discovered that what was important to me was important to God. He cared about how I was feeling, what I was thinking, what I wanted for myself and for my children. God wanted to share things with me as well. He wanted to show me how He had been victorious in the lives of those He had called and anointed, how He had performed miracles in the lives of those who followed Him and believed in Him. Reading the Bible stopped feeling like a chore and started feeling like a privilege.

A big lesson I had to learn was not to use the Word as a tool to manipulate God into doing what I wanted Him to do, as if God can be manipulated. I had to learn that the purpose of reading the Word was to deepen my relationship with God. Growing in the wisdom of the Word and the statutes of the Almighty was the greatest reward.

The next step in this new life was to make prayer a natural, effortless part of my life. Now, this took some work. Throughout my life, prayer had been ritualistic and filled with religious rhetoric, either mumbled incoherently or shouted, as if God was hard of hearing. I had grown up listening to deacons, elders, Mother's Board, singing Dr. Watts. For all the white people and non-southern blacks, get a black Baptist person from the South to explain this to you (smile). After these Dr. Watts, church folk would go into these prayer monologues that contain a certain rhythm and phraseology—the greater the phrasing, the greater the prayer. And I could pray 'em with the best phraseologist. I had plenty of spark, but no fire.

I had to learn how to just get quiet with God—how to talk to Him and how to let Him talk to me. Since God is a God of relationships, I had to learn how to relate to God. To be naked (soulishly) before God and share what was in my heart and to hear what was in His heart for me was harder than everything else I had done up to that point.

This step required honesty. My trust in God was a newly re-established connection, but being honest with God and being accountable for my choices stung a little bit. It was hard to face up to what a huge mess I had made of my life. Even though the volatile catalyst to my destruction had been added in by others, there had been many, many, many times when God had placed people in my life to show me a better way. I just ignored them. I liked holding on to my security blanket that was soaked in dysfunction because it was all

I knew. It is like being a slave for a large portion of your life and then someone coming along and saying, "Okay, you are free now. Go and be happy." Where do you go? What do you do? In all likelihood, you sell yourself back into slavery because you do not know how to be free. And that is exactly what I did. Freedom was too much. I had stayed a slave way too long. Now it was time to learn how to be free.

Soon after that I began to use my long dormant gift of being Spirit-filled and then there was no going back. I began to look forward to my time with God. I anticipated getting away and sharing intimate time with God daily. I could hear God. I could feel God. It was a wonderful, new, exciting, thrilling experience. I had never had a relationship with God like the one I had now. It is breathtaking.

The
Promised
Land

Do Over

I was feeling good about myself. My life was going very well. I was working at the church. I was back on my feet, living in my own apartment, ready to move on with my life. I was happy with the direction my life was going. My only regret was that I had done all this growing and changing and my husband had not been a part of it. He was living with his girlfriend, the one he had moved in with when I was pregnant with our son. I had moved to the other side of the apartment complex we all lived in and had gotten an apartment of my own where I was living with our two children. My husband had gone through with the divorce and I did not fight him on it.

Our divorce became final in August of 2000. Once final, he continued to live with his girlfriend, and I lived alone and carried the responsibility of caring for the kids. My (now ex) husband still refused to help me financially and I could not fully afford the cost of their daycare on my own. During the frustration of carrying that responsibility alone, I dropped our children off at their apartment one day and I told him that I would pick them up every Thursday afternoon and return them to him every Monday morning. We shared our children equally for about the first six months. Since I didn't fight for any of my rights during the divorce proceedings, he requested and was awarded physical custody and I was ordered to pay child support. Shortly afterward, I was given primary care of our children. I was off government assistance and could now take care of them.

In that first year following our divorce, I had changed tremendously and was becoming a woman I could be proud of—and oddly enough, a woman my (now ex) husband had become attracted to all over again—or so I thought. My husband and I began talking about putting our family back together. He started saying how he could see the positive effect LWBC was having on my life since our divorce. We began seeing each other, despite the fact that he was still living with his girlfriend. Since we were now divorced, she began to talk about the two of them getting married, but he would not entertain the thought.

Soon he began to share with me how he wanted his family back together, how he missed me and the children. He loved the new Dionne who didn't argue, prayed a lot, was more gentle and kind, not stressed out. He could see that I was truly happy and he wanted to be a part of it. He wanted to move in together. I told him that I could not live

> I had changed tremendously and was becoming a woman I could be proud of.

with him and not be married to him. Where I was in God prevented me from making that choice. His response was, "So let's get married again."

Our divorce was final in August of 2000 and we were remarried in July of 2001. I remember the look on the faces of my pastors. It looked like a Lord-please-help-us-all-get-through-this kinda look. My husband started attending church with me. The church took him in and accepted him right away, despite their own reservations. A church member even gave him a job with his company, with perks like the use of one of his cars, which my husband wrecked one day going to a job site.

In my mind, our remarriage was a chance for me to be accountable for what I had done wrong during our first marriage and go back and get it right. I was determined that we would be a family after God's own heart. We would raise our children together in the admonition of God. We would grow old together, hand in hand. Me, my man, and God would form an unbeatable team. The harsh reality was that only I had become rooted and grounded in the Word of God. My relationship with God had deepened and solidified. I had grown; we had not.

We were both working full time jobs. We had moved into this large tri-level house, the house of my dreams. My husband did a lot of work to fix the house up. He even threw me a surprise birthday party with all of my friends from the church. I thought things were going well. I was paying all the house bills and he was supposed to be paying the house rent. We were consistently late with the payments and several months after we moved in we were evicted. But not before the owner of the home had gotten a judgment against us for the money we owed him. I was consumed with worry about our debt situation coupled with the fact that I did not have a clear understanding of what was going on. Where was our money going? Why was my husband so unfocused?

After the house eviction, in late 2001, my husband lost his job and moved us into a small two bedroom apartment. I was still working at the church. He had changed jobs and was now working for another church member.

In early 2002, my husband's father died and he went into a severe depression and started drinking heavily. Since we'd partied together years before, I wouldn't say I liked it, but it really didn't bother me. Since there were no longer any drugs involved, I wasn't too concerned.

During this time we'd both leave in the morning for work. I thought he was going to work, but he would come back home, hang out, go fishing, and not work for days at a time. His employer and now friend wanted to be his mentor. He understood my husband in ways no other man had ever understood him. This man reached out to my husband in every way he could, not just monetarily, but one man reaching out to help save another. My husband could not see it and would not except it. After we returned from his father's funeral in

Louisiana, he became more distant and more unfocused. He stopped attending church with me and the children. He was always either too tired, didn't feel good, or whatever other excuse he could come up with.

By March of 2002, we were evicted from this apartment. My children and I moved in with my mother—in hiding. She lived in a retirement community with a roommate and wasn't supposed to have guests for more than three consecutive days. She and her roommate let us hide out in their small home for more than three weeks. I did not know where my husband was staying, but he would come by to see me and the children. We would have to sneak into our apartment for clothes and other belongings.

Through all of this, God had not forsaken me. I didn't tell the Andersons that we had been evicted. With everything they were teaching me and all they were pouring into me, I could not bring myself to tell them what was going on. In my mind, they would have said what I was thinking to myself, "I told you so." What had possessed me to believe what my husband was telling me? What in the world was I thinking when

I remarried him? I had worked hard to remain unwavering and faithful.

The church member my husband was working for at the time overheard me talking to my mother and figured out that we were living with her. When he found out why, he paid all of our back rent, fees, and paid our rent for one month forward. On my husband's birthday, April 4, 2002 he got a phone call from

> We thought we were going to be summoned to court or arrested or something.

his mother telling him the apartment complex was looking for him. She told him he needed to call the apartment office right away. He called me and we didn't know if we should call them or avoid them. We thought we were going to be summoned to court or arrested or something, but his mother said the news was good.

The apartment manager told us someone had come by and paid everything for us and we could move back in whenever we wanted to. I immediately started thanking and praising God for the greatest financial miracle I had seen in my life up to that point. I was quick to point out to my husband how God had blessed us, how

God had covered us. In spite of ourselves, God had provided for us as only He can. When we reentered our apartment, all of our belongings were right where we had left them a month before. Despite God's provision, thirty days later, we were right back in the same predicament facing another eviction.

I did not know it at the time, but my husband had maintained a friendship with the girlfriend he had shared an apartment with previously (Woman #3) and had a new girlfriend (Woman #4) as well. Now facing eviction again, my husband talked about moving back to Louisiana as a way to get away, start over. He said he wanted a fresh start with people who really supported him, instead of people he claimed were out to get him. This whole scene sounded much like that one that had brought us out to Arizona ten years earlier.

I remember one evening in particular, around May of 2002, when his sister invited me to her apartment for dinner. She and her husband were living in the same apartment complex as we were at the time. She said there was something I needed to see. She said when she was ready for me to come over, she would call me. We had concocted a story about her husband needing an airline buddy pass to travel back to Louisiana and I was to come over, explaining that I had tried to get one, but couldn't. She said that what she wanted to show me, I wouldn't believe unless I saw it with my own eyes.

I kept asking her what could possibly be so important or earth-shattering. She tried to tell me about a woman (Woman #4) who had come to her job looking for my husband and how the young woman explained that she had a relationship with my husband. I refused to believe his sister and accused her of making it up. She also told me that my husband had maintained a friendship with his ex-girlfriend (Woman #3) and had brought her over to his sister's home on a couple of occasions while I was home caring for our children.

When I walked into their apartment the night she called me, I walked into what looked like a scene from a cheesy soap opera. The young lady he once shared an apartment with (Woman #3) was sitting on the couch in the living room. My husband was hiding behind the door. His sister was standing in the din-

ing room. Her husband was sitting at the dining room table and his mother was sitting in a
chair in the living room.

As I walked in, I was completely stunned
at what I saw. When I thought it couldn't get
any worse, my husband's sister looked over
to my husband and asked him, "Who is this
one?" and another woman (Woman #4) came
out from one of the bedrooms. To my dismay,
this woman had been to my home looking for
my husband earlier that week, claiming that
he was helping her with some landscaping.
She had even been to the church weeks earlier
looking for me to talk to me, but left before we
talked. The three of us, one apartment—and
front-row seating to the show for the immedi-
ate family.

My husband ran out. I left and went
home to pack some things so I could get
away that night and clear my head. I was
confused and dazed a bit. I recall shedding
a few tears, but I was not devastated. Over
those last several months with my husband,
many things seemed out of sorts. The shock
was in seeing it with my own eyes, showing me what I believe I already knew in my
heart to be true.

My spirit had heard from God, so this scene was not as devastating as it would have been years ago. God had grown me up enough and was talking to me enough to know that my choices were my own and my husband's choices were his own, each choice coming with its rewards or consequences as mandated by the individual choice.

> My spirit had heard from God, so this scene was not as devastating as it would have been years ago.

My mistake in all of this was to face it with reason and religiosity. My husband, in my mind, obviously had a problem, a stronghold in his life. I thought all he needed was time and prayer to be delivered from all of this. I could and would try to pray him better, but I would not leave his side. What I ignored was the truth that his own choices had brought him here, not an all out attack of the enemy or the scapegoats of his upbringing and the past. It had all been a matter of free will choice.

In July of 2002, my husband decided we should move back to Louisiana. He moved me and our children in with a girlfriend of mine from church. A girlfriend who had been there for me through all of this mess, not a girlfriend in the modern-day sense of the word, but the ol' school definition, somebody who has your back and loves you. She didn't say, "I told you so," or ridicule me for standing by my husband. She just welcomed me into her home with open arms. She told me that no matter what, she was there for me, whether I decided to leave or stay. She just wanted me to be happy.

During this time, my children and I lived in one of her bedrooms in a small house she shared with her two daughters. One of her daughters moved out of her bedroom and gave it to me and my children. My children and I shared a small bedroom with a bunk bed and a television. My children slept on the top bunk and I slept on the bottom. We all had access to the living and dining room, as well as the kitchen.

My husband was supposed to come back and get us in September of that same year. The church had thrown a huge going away party for me and given me a huge send off. My pastors brought me before the congregation and blessed me to go and be with my husband. Pastor Maureen bought me a digital camera as a going away present. She pulled me to the side shortly before I was supposed to leave and said, "Use this camera so I can see where you are living and how you are living, so I can know you are okay." I agreed to her request, resigned my position and went to my girlfriend's house to wait for my husband.

September came and went and October was almost gone. My husband had not come to get me. Past torments showed up to talk to me and mock me in my stand for my marriage. All that came from my husband were excuses as to why he had not sent us any money or come to get us. He spoke of hurricanes that prevented him from working. He claimed to have found us a home and bought me a car.

I would call his uncle in Louisiana almost daily, trying to reach my husband and talk to him. Finally, after weeks of this, my husband's uncle, who knew I had quit my job, told me I'd better call the church and see if I could get my job back. He did not specify why or tell me what was going on out there, he just told me that I had a good job and I should probably stay where I was, that if I came, it might not end up being what I thought it was going to be.

I would later learn that my husband had taken his demons with him and was already having another affair with a young lady there (Woman #5). This woman even knew about me and my children and thought my husband and I were divorced. During this time, I had a death in my family and had to travel back to Louisiana. My husband told his current girlfriend that he had to come and meet me in West Monroe and take care of our children while I went to the funeral. I had not brought my children with me. My husband came to the funeral and stood by my side. I thought it was to support me; it was really to pacify me to continue to believe him, go back to Arizona and wait for him to come.

My girlfriend, who I was still living with when I returned from the funeral, had taken care of us over the last couple of months. I was getting by on what little savings I had left, with no monetary support from my husband. My girlfriend told me that if I needed to stay, I could, but that I needed to get up and go to work and quit sulking. She said she was tired of watching me wait at her door like a dog waiting for its owner at the end of a long day. Well, I was still waiting and no one had come to claim me or my little puppies.

The church had no idea I had never moved away. I was too embarrassed to call them and tell them the truth and I had not stepped foot into the church since the week I was supposed to leave almost two months earlier. I finally called Pastor Maureen and she talked to Pastor Tom. I told her I didn't expect to come back to the church to work or otherwise, that it would be too hard, too embarrassing. I just wanted her to know I was still in town. In my heart, I wanted to find a way to come back to the church without glaring eyes, intrusive questions and the scrutiny of thousands of people. Remember, I wasn't supposed to be there.

> She said she was tired of watching me wait at her door like a dog waiting for its owner.

My pastors offered to find me a job. What they really did was to create a job at the church for me. Their sons, who run the ministry and are like my brothers, were a bit skeptical of my return at first. One of my spiritual brothers, Scot, asked me, "We are done with all of this aren't we?" He said he couldn't go through this with me again. They were more hurt for me than I was over what had happened, but each of them said they were not surprised.

I knew this was not God's fault, so I didn't waste His time asking how or why. I didn't waste time blaming Him. I knew who, how and why—free will served on a cold platter with a side of ripe bad choices and a large hater'ade. My pastors understood better than I did how getting me back in church would be critical to sustaining the growth that had occurred in me over the last few years. They didn't want to see me change direction and walk away from God because my marriage didn't go the way I thought it would. I came back to work at the church in early November of 2002.

Again Jesus interceded on my behalf. There was a townhouse for rent right down the street from the church. I spoke to the owner and was very honest with him. I told him I was separated from my husband and trying to get back on my feet and I was going back to college. We met. He ran my credit and laughed. He said based on that alone, I would not qualify for the townhouse, but he said there was something about me that he just couldn't get away from. He said he wanted to give me a chance and would allow me to rent his place against his own better judgment, according to business standards. But I knew it was God allowing this man to see my heart and not my credit report. A couple at the church gave me money to pay the deposit on the townhouse. It was God start to finish!

My children and I moved into our own townhouse just before Thanksgiving of 2002. That year, we had a lot to be thankful for. I kept quietly telling God that I was so afraid that I could not make it on my own. God spoke to me with this revelation: I had been "making" it on my own for many, many years, but definitely not alone. God began to step in and take on the role of husband in my life and was teaching me how to be a good mother to my children.

Divorce Revisited

In January of 2003, my husband was moving back to Arizona from Louisiana and asked if he could live with me and our children. Since we were still legally married, I agreed. I bought him a plane ticket to come back to Arizona. Shortly after his return, he had rekindled a relationship with a previous girlfriend (Woman #4), who was now dating one of his good friends. My legal husband was now living with me and hiding the fact he was seeing her, living between both homes at the same time. He told me he had gotten a job four days a week in Tucson, so he could be home with me and our children during the week, but he would leave "for work" (wink, wink) every weekend.

My children had met his girlfriend and had spent time with her and her children. She had even been to my townhouse when I wasn't home. My husband was telling her this fantastic story of how he owned his own company and had given me the townhouse so his children would have a place to live, even if it meant he would have to live somewhere else. He told her that the car he was driving at the time (my car), he had bought for me so the kids and I would have transportation. He had answers for every question she or I posed to him.

I prayed and asked God for wisdom and I asked him for clarity. I asked God to allow me to see my husband's infidelity just as plainly as I see the words on this page. It sounds like an odd request, one of those "what's the matter with you, girl, it's been happening right in front of your face, you can't see the forest for the trees." I was consumed with staying married, being a good Christian wife, you know the routine, having done all to stand, standing therefore, the unbelieving husband is sanctified by the wife, longsuffering—you know.

God had already shown me that my husband's heart had grown cold and selfish. There was an emptiness; an endless void never being filled. All the women in his life were fillers. Our marriage had become like sand being poured into a vase with a slotted bottom. My husband's thirst could not be satisfied because he was drinking temporal water of earthen vessels, not the living water of the Word of God. The Word talks about a man who had once known God and the things of God and walked away from them. It tells of the man's torment being greater and it would have been better for the man had he never known God in the first place.

After God began to speak to me about my husband, I asked God to let me see my husband through my spiritual eyes. The only hope for him and for me would be to let my husband go to do what was in his heart to do. I began to guard my heart from his words and his actions. I began to see plainly how his life had been formulated by his upbringing and environment, but had been fueled as an adult by his own internal fire that raged against the Spirit of God within him. There was nothing I could do to help him or save him. That price had already been paid. It was not my sacrifice to make. I stopped pleading my case as to why we should be together.

> In February of that year, we went out for the last time together as husband and wife.

In February of that year, we went out for the last time together as husband and wife. He took me to the theatre for Valentine's Day and bought me a birthstone necklace and earring set. It was something he had promised to do long ago. I have no idea why out of all the promises he made to me, year after year, this would be one of the few he ever kept. I will probably never know.

In March of 2003, he moved in with his then girlfriend (Woman #4). She became pregnant in July or August of 2003. The Lord had shown me she was going to get pregnant. I shared with my husband what God had shown me and he dispelled it saying that I was over there in "those stupid @#$% domes (LWBC), with all those white people, speaking in tongues and letting the Laud show 'em stuff." He didn't believe me; he mocked me and made fun of me. I even told him that God had shown me that it would be a girl, which he didn't believe either.

I asked my husband to file for divorce, since he was the one who was already with someone else. He told me that he paid for the first one and he was already with the woman he wanted to be with. If I wanted a divorce, he felt like I should pay for it. He told me he wouldn't contest it, but he wouldn't contribute to it either. Divorce was NEVER what I wanted to do, but I had no other choice. God had given me peace about filing. I filed for divorce in August of 2003. Our divorce was final in January of 2004. My now former husband and his then girlfriend (Woman #4) gave birth to their daughter in April of 2004 and were married in September of that same year.

I looked at my children and knew the decision I had made to file for divorce was what I had to do for all of us, not just me. One of the deciding factors for me was the day my son, who was about five at the time, asked me, "Mommy, when I get married, can I have a girlfriend, like Daddy?" I politely said no and went into my room and cried.

> My son, who was about five at the time, asked me, "Mommy, when I get married, can I have a girlfriend like Daddy?"

What was I teaching my children? I was teaching my daughter to accept less than God's absolute best for her life. I had shown her she should be under the spiritual covering of a man living outside of the will of God. I was teaching her to pursue a man and then hold on to him at all cost. I was teaching my son that it is okay to disrespect the gift that a woman is created to be

to a man. I was not teaching him to love and es-
teem and treasure one wife. I was allowing him
to see that one woman is not enough. These
were not the life lessons I had planned on teaching my children.

Even if I wanted to sacrifice my life and
stay in this facade of a marriage, I could not
sacrifice my children to repeat this cycle of
dysfunction all over again when they become
adults. I had to take authority over this generational curse. This stronghold had to end with
me. The reason I believe God had given me a
son was because I had asked God for a son. I
promised God I would raise my son to love God
above all else. My son would change the lin-
eage of my husband's family back to covenant
with God and the things of God. God had heard
my request and gave me a son. And I kept my
promise to God and I am raising my son and my
daughter to love God above all else.

Jokingly, by now, I felt like the only thing
I was good at was being divorced. I had become
an accidental expert. I was angry for awhile. I
am not sure if I was angrier at myself, or angrier
with my now former husband. I pondered the
concept that he only remarried me to get back at
me and punish me for what he felt was my be-

trayal. Was he ever really committed to making our second marriage work, or did he just want to shame and humiliate me? I decided that I was expending too much useful energy on questions I will never get the answers to. It was over and I needed to let it be over. I needed to move on and rejoice over my new life. Now my life would have no limits.

My spiritual mom and dad (Pastors Tom and Maureen) told me they did not think remarrying my husband was a good idea because both of us were not committed to making it work. They shared with me that since I was so adamant about reconciliation, they had no right to try to force me not to; they would not go against the prime directive of free will. I had the God–given right to choose to go back and, as my parents, they supported my right to choose.

Honestly, looking back at it now, I do not think I would have learned what I learned had I not gone back. I got to use all the skills I had learned when we were divorced the first time. I fasted, I prayed, I talked, I listened, I trusted God. Although, it had not worked out the way I thought it would, I trusted God and God had not let me down. God protected me and covered me in spite of everything. The lessons I learned during that do over have been invaluable to my ministry and my life.

I also walked away knowing wholeheartedly and soul-ly understanding why God hates divorce, but put an allowance for it in His Word. When I left that marriage the second time, I knew down to the very depths of my being that I had done everything in my power to stay married. By earning my way out, I was able to leave with no hurt, shame, guilt, or bitterness. Nothing was left undone. Let me make myself very clear, I DO NOT ADVOCATE DIVORCE. I HATE DIVORCE, unless there is no other choice.

For the nights I wept, God was right there with me, wiping my tears. For the days I spent trying to figure out what was wrong with me, God was there comforting me. For the moments I struggled with my own self worth, God whispered to me to look around and see how He had surrounded me with His love. For the moments I wondered about my destiny, He reminded me how He had continuously redirected me back to His will time and time again. For moments I doubted if I was doing the right thing, He showed me how even though my marriage had fallen apart, my life had not.

In His Word, God promises to work all things out for my good because I am called according to His purpose. God's plans for me are for good; plans not to harm me, but to prosper me, to give me a hope and a future. This fire that the enemy ignited to destroy me, fanned by my own wrong choices and fueled by my husband's insatiable desires, God used to forge a stronger, wiser, more well-equipped Dionne. I have not looked back since!

Life After Divorce

I must say though that no one could tell me when enough was enough. No one could have told me to stay longer or leave sooner. I know I would not have listened. God knew I had endured enough long before I did and long before I would listen to (even) Him giving me permission to leave. It wasn't until I knew I had done all I could to do, no more could be done—"Doctor, the patient is dead."

The hardest part of divorce is that it truly represents a death. A covenant has been broken and a death has occurred, but there is no body to bury. The person you divorce is a living reminder of perceived failure, for both of you. Bishop T. D. Jakes once taught that there are only two reasons for any divorce. "One spouse wouldn't forgive or one spouse wouldn't repent." Either way, it's over and life must begin again. God doesn't break covenant, we do. It is so important to be very careful who you enter into covenant with. It is a very serious matter that I had taken way too lightly. And by the time I did take it seriously, it was way too late.

The only ache in my heart with regard to going through the divorce was the toll it has taken on my children. Had there been another road to take, I would have found it. Although, I never wanted my children to grow up in a single-parent home, I more so didn't want my son to become his father or my daughter to marry a man like her father, at least not the man he is now. Furthermore, I knew I owed them a better life than my past. I now strive to find the balance between all the privilege that I grew up with, coupled with a knowledge and dependence on God, and the fellowship of the Holy Spirit. I have taught my children to pray and hear from God. They know how to discern the anointing. I have taught them how to plead the blood of Jesus over their family and friends, and to dispatch their angels to protect and watch over them.

I realize my children have paid a much higher price than their father or I. I know now that I did them a greater disservice by remarrying their father, given that the first divorce was easier on them because of their ages. The second divorce was much harder, more emotional for them. It is like having a scar that is partly healed, reopening the wound and pouring anti-septic in it. It hurts worse. They have had challenges in school, emotional challenges, anger challenges, and be-havioral challenges.

> I realize my children have paid a much higher price than their father or I.

From bedwetting to fighting to lashing out to crying spells, we've been through it all.

My children and I have had a very open relationship as far as talking about the divorce and allowing them the time to process their anger and deal with their sense of loss. They had no control over this situation and no in-put about getting divorced or staying together. My children's feelings of helplessness, a nor-mal part of childhood, were only amplified in a negative way by our divorce.

My children and I have all been through extensive counseling to help us process all of this and walk victoriously out of it. Two of the wisest things I did for them and for me is to teach the skill of learning to hear from God and getting mentors. I learned to pray over the simplest of decisions because I had lost my sense of security in making my own decisions and my confidence that those decisions would be the right ones. My children are both Spirit-filled and I have tried to instill in them that if they pray over the decisions they make and wait to hear from God, the likelihood of making a godly choice goes up exponentially.

Since their sense of security was found in me and their father and we had jacked that up, it was now my responsibility to show them how to depend on something, someone greater than me, who would NEVER let them down. This was a skill I did not have as a child, thus the first section of the book. Now, let's be real. They are children, so they fight, they argue, they play, they take each other's stuff. They are not super spiritual—they are kids. But that constant reminder from me to lean on God is regularly playing in the background music of their lives and I pray will usher them into a bright future.

The other wise thing I did for my children was to find married mentors for each of them. These are couples who have godly marriages, who my children can spend time with.

My children get the opportunity to see godly, healthy, loving interactions between married couples and their children. I chose each couple after a lot of prayer and fasting, since these couples would be allowed to speak into my children's lives. But I will explain that in depth in the next book (smile).

For myself, I have committed to being mentored by my pastors and I have a covenant relationship with my intercessor. My pastors and their sons have a unique position in my life as my spiritual parents and siblings. I have submitted myself to them to learn from them and be guided by them. I also am voluntarily accountable to them both professionally and personally and I allow them to speak into my life.

God also put me in relationship with an intercessor, who is also my most cherished friend. She prays for me and comes into agreement with me in ministry and in all aspects of my personal life. She allows me to be at my best as well as my worst, but is faithful to always help me navigate back to God. She helps me navigate through my occasional circular journey that starts with God and ends with God, but with some human ranting and raving (mine) and a little hissy fit in the middle. And then of course I relent and do what God told me to do in the first place. Am I the only one here who does that? Probably not. Everyone needs the kind of friend who lets you have your moment, but is quick to slap you back into shape when you need it. Everyone needs one friend like that in his or her life. To hear it from her, she always tells me how much she learns from me. I jokingly respond, "Yeah, what not to do in ten easy steps, as taught by Dionne," we both just laugh. She says the changes I've made in my life by the leading of the Holy Spirit have inspired her. Honestly, the changes I have made have truly amazed me. Had I known where I could have been in God, I would have died to my junk and let it all go a long time ago.

My happiness is not founded on material things. Thank God my definition of who I am is no longer wrapped up in someone else's opinion of me. Glory be to God that my future is no longer burning on the altar of my past, sending up smoke signals of a life that could have been. I am alive and well, I know who I am in Christ, and I know who Christ is in me. If anyone had told me seven years ago where my life would be now, I would have sworn we did drugs together in the late 80s. My life today is so far from my childhood, so far from my young adulthood, it is as if I have been given a whole new life. That's right, I have been given a new life.

So When Does Life Get Good?

I would be lying if I said that after my divorce the sky opened, a heavenly choir began to sing "The storm is passing over" and everything was good. It was not all good. The enemy still came and tried to convince me that I would never be usable for ministry, that I was tainted, soiled, unworthy. If I were to write every word the enemy spoke to me, this would have been a book of letters from the enemy to the village idiot.

Sometimes you just have to laugh at the enemy. I have to admit, he tried his best. It was a valiant effort, but he failed, Praise God! Same old tired tricks that he has used for thousands of years is what trips us up every time. When I learned to see what was really going on, it reduced the enemy down to a well-polished magician performing cheap parlor tricks. My father God is so much stronger and mightier than him. I was finally able to walk out of this self-imposed prison and go enjoy my life. I was sitting in a prison with the door open, too scared to walk out the door and into life and freedom.

This time I didn't try to fight the enemy on his own terms. I didn't beat myself up arguing with the enemy over what I did versus what my former husband did. It took two of us to get married and two of us to get divorced. That was not arguable. But what I did tell the enemy was that I would no longer be categorized by my past. I would be walking according to my destiny. I fought him with the Word of God, like Jesus did when He was tempted. The enemy hates that, you know! I took on Jesus' righteousness and the grace of God. I welcomed every morning that was already filled with the new mercies of God, Hallelujah. The bonds that used to hold me like slave shackles now seemed foolish and weightless—no stronger than thread tied to the leg of a lioness.

MY LIFE GOT GOOD; WHEN I DECIDED IT WAS GOOD! God gave me an incredible job, a nice and safe home for me and my children. God surrounded me with a church family who loved me and celebrated me. And He gave me (spiritual) parents to be accountable to and to help me learn and grow. I told God I wanted to experience real love, and all I had to do was look around me. I was surrounded by love, acceptance, value, adoration, appreciation, peace, favor and an unending source of blessings.

The biggest challenge to walking in the promises of God was my own doubt and unbelief of not being worthy of the life I have now. Walking out of the prison paled in comparison to stepping out into true freedom. I felt like

> This time I didn't try to fight the enemy on his own terms.

a prisoner walking out of a cell, down the corridor, out the yard, past the gate and out to freedom. It was those last few steps that seemed the hardest to make. At times I was tempted to look back, go back to prison where I felt safe, where I knew what was on the menu and what my job assignments were.

My dysfunction had been my only security blanket and God was showing me that He wanted me to be happy, healthy and successful, dependent on Him and Him alone, not being pacified by my dysfunction. When you and I learn to walk in victory, we become a threat to the enemy because we can tell others how to walk that same path.

I had to forgive myself, let go of my past and take on the unconditional love of God. I had to let go of everything and everyone who hindered me from seeing myself the way God sees me. Taking on His vision of me has been a wonderful journey. Learning to love who I am, learning why He created me, has been an awesome time of fellowshipping with God. When storms come, and they have (and they will), it is up to me to remember that Jesus is in the boat with me, I am not alone. If need be, He will come up to the top of the boat and command peace to my storm.

Listen to me. Each of us is called to greatness. Our greatness can be outwardly visible, such as ministering throughout the country for God, or it can be outwardly invisible such as raising the next Nobel Peace Prize award winner. Either way, we are called to do something awesome that will leave a lasting effect in our community and in our nation. It is the invisible that commands the visible.

What I am saying is we focus so much attention on what we can see, touch, smell, hear, taste. What makes the eternal difference is not those things at all. It is what we cannot see that ushers us into the presence of God and ultimately to walking according to His will. Those tangible elements are what you see after the non-tangibles have done their jobs. For instance, you want to be a good spouse, it takes more than the marriage license hanging on your wall or tucked in the back of a drawer of your home office. What will set you apart as a spouse is a commitment to building and maintaining a covenant marriage, which requires your full participation in the love walk, partnered up with faith and prayer, along with a refreshing drink of the living water of the Word. The results of these things being actively at work within you will make you a spouse who doesn't cheat, doesn't lie, and doesn't accept less than God's best in your marriage.

When I looked inward and allowed God to restore those important elements of my character, I realized they were in there lying dormant all along, hidden under betrayal, rejection, hurt, and abuse. There was a good person inside of me, a godly person well able to make godly decisions, now becoming equipped to affect my world positively and help build the kingdom of God. I was usable. I wasn't trash. I wasn't disposable. God can use me to show others the way and to show others that with God you can overcome anything.

On the following page is an excerpt from the first poem I wrote after the journey back to God began. God used to speak to me all the time through my poems and writings. Since I was not willing to listen to Him any other way, He simply used the talent He gave me to speak to me. Back in 1998, God spoke to me in one of my poems and tried to forewarn me about things to come, but I wouldn't listen. After it all came true, I stopped writing. In the poem below, God spoke to me for the first time in my writings since 1998. In it, God stressed to me the importance of free will and that what the enemy was really selling me was a bag of worthless goods.

What will come, will come,

What will be, will be?

NO!

God gave me a unique gift, Free Will—

I choose to agree with God, **OR** to agree with nothing…

What will come is in fact ~ What I call forth,

I speak nothing, I get nothing.

And nothing is hand delivered by the devil.

Father of all lies, hider of all truth

WHO

Came from nothing

Owns nothing

Offers nothing,

Promising that which he has not.

In essence

Yes **I WILL** or no **I WILL NOT!**

MY will is now **Thy** will,

Truth

Life

Abundance,

Favor,

Faith,

Love,

and Blessings

that overtake me;

if **I WILL,**

if **I WILL NOT,** Surely no[thing] will come.

(Written January 2003)

Getting Good at Being Single

I do not know of any little girl who grows up, dreaming of being a single mom. I know I didn't. I had to face the fact that life brought me to a point where I was a single mom. It was up to me to choose whether or not I was going to be defined by being a statistic. I determined in my heart to be a single mom among single moms. I would learn how to lean and depend on God as my husband. I would teach my children to love God above all else and learn to pray about every life-altering decision they make. I would learn to live, laugh, and love the way God intended it. And I would surrender my life to Him wholly, to do with as He pleases.

What I love about being single is that it gave me the opportunity to focus on my relationship with God above all else and then build a healthy relationship with my children. Through this whole experience, I learned that I did not love Dionne and I did not trust God.

At this point I can honestly say, today I love who I am. I am not perfect, but my imperfections come from a heart that loves God and I am striving daily to reflect Him more and more in my life. As far as my relationship with God goes, I trust Him with my life. I made a God-led decision to completely surrender every aspect of my life over to Him and allow Him to speak to me as to what direction I go in, the choices I make. I didn't find God. He chose me and I said, "Yes!"

God is teaching me how to love from a pure place, a God place. Granted, loving is difficult, but very rewarding. I thought I was little more than a mishap; that somehow I had been born outside of the will and plan of God. That was a lie from the pit of Hell. I have learned that God wanted me to be born, needed me to be born and gave me a unique destiny to fulfill. My life is unlike that of anyone else.

Another great part of being single is that God has helped me unpack and get rid of so much baggage. If I hadn't, someone else was bound to get hit with the fallout. What made me such a good spokeswoman of doom in my life was all the junk I was carrying around with me in my designer Louis Doom luggage. When we have baggage that we take from relationship to relationship, we unpack certain items and leave them behind. Then we add to our baggage in that relationship and carry it on with us into the next relationship.

Well, God has been able to take me aside and say, "Dionne, we are going to have to unpack some stuff if you are going to be healthy and whole" (not literally, but figuratively). My response, like most human beings was, "But God, I really like that. It looks so good on me. Can I keep it?" We have emotional bags packed full of stuff—old hurts, offense, bitterness, anger, etc. There's God trying to help us unpack and empty the bags in order to make our walk with Him lighter. Remember, His yoke is easy and His burden is light. It is our own yoke, our own burdens that weigh us down so heavily.

When it comes to marriage, I believe it can be a love story when God writes it. I married my soul mate and that is exactly why we are divorced. If you believe in your soul lives the mind, the will and the emotions, then they may not be the best meter reader by which to gauge the validity or compatibility of a potential mate. These facets of who we are are volatile and unpredictable. They definitely change with age, environment, climate, culture, just to name a few catalysts. We (women) are infamous for changing our minds (right, men) and don't even get me started on us and our emotions (right, ladies). I need to choose my mate by the Spirit of the Living God, who dwells within me. I want to marry my spirit-mate. I want to be able to serve and love God together. I want to be able to pray and fast together, to cover each other. I want to be able to come under his covering as the man of the house, a man after God's own heart. I want a love story! And guess what? I will have one!

Conclusion

It is my prayer that this book ministered to every reader in a unique and special way. I know some of you have read this book and cannot relate to my story at all. If you know you have a good husband, celebrate him, tell him, love him and thank God for him. This book was not for you. Honestly, I thank God for you and for the fact that you have never been through anything like this, so please give this book to your girlfriend—you know, the one who will be blessed by it, the one who needs it.

There have been others who have read this book and will find uncanny similarities in our experiences and you are just happy to know that you are not alone. Well, you are not. And if I can make it, so can you. I pray my story has inspired you. This is me extending my shoulder for you to cry on. It is my way of saying, "It's going to be okay, girl. Get up. Wipe the dirt off of you and keep moving forward."

Then there are still others of you who have read this book and said, "Honey, you ain't been through nothing. You should hear my story." To you I say, let God heal you and put you on the road to better living, if He hasn't already. Get Better, Get Out, or Get Over It, but you have to pick one. Otherwise you are stagnant, and whatever does not continue to grow, is already dead.

I do not want to become the poster woman for every woman who wants a divorce. In case you missed it, I HATE DIVORCE! No one in his or her right mind who marries the same person twice wants to be divorced. I left having spilled blood, sweat, and tears. I am only one woman trying to show someone else that the prison door is not locked. It's really open. You've had the key all the time. Freedom is waiting just on the other side of an open door.

A Note From the Author

I am a culmination of all those things be-hind me and all the things around me now. I do not want anyone who reads this book to be in judgment against me or in awe of me. I am just a real person, who suffered some real hardships and managed to get on the other side. I am showing you my wounds, in the hope that it will help you heal. I pray this book serves as a reminder to all of us of the endearing and enduring perseverance of God to not give up on any of us. He certainly never gave up on me.

It is God's redemption and love that rescued me and set my life on the path to a great future. It is God's mercy and grace that pursued me in my own darkness, and Jesus who interceded for me to come out of that darkness and into the light of His amazing love. I am not adequately built to be able to properly proclaim who God is to me or properly relay to you the immeasurable value of what He has done in my life and through my life. It is my humble prayer that as people meet me, hear me, see me, interact with me—it becomes clearly and vis-ibly evident.

Dionne Arceneaux

Acknowledgments

I thank God for allowing me to be angry with Him over my divorce and I thank God for the grace to get on the other side of those emotions, knowing that He hated my divorce as much as I did. I thank Him for my life and for being a God of second chances. I love you, Lord!

I thank God for my mother, Julia Houston, who literally prayed me to Living Word Bible Church and did not reap a harvest on those prayers for six years. The prayers of the righteous really do avail much. Thanks, Mom.

I thank God for my spiritual parents, Dr. C. Thomas and Pastor Maureen Anderson, who loved me and mentored me into the person I am now. My life is forever changed because of you. Thank you for seeing in me what I could not see in myself. Their sons, my spiritual brothers, Scot and Jason, thank you for holding me accountable for my actions and teaching me to walk in the fullness of God, to want and require more from my life than the mediocre. Thank you for showing me how to live according to my destiny.

A special note to Mr. Tyler Perry, who talked about writing being cathartic for him. He inspired me (a homegirl) to write my story without second guessing myself. If God and writing helped him heal, it has certainly done the same for me. Thank you for your courage and honesty. It's hard being this exposed and real. Thanks for doing it first.

I thank God for all my church family, family back home, and friends worldwide who have watched me grow in the Lord and been just as amazed as I am. Thanks to Holly Sitzler for an awesome book cover. Thanks to Cynthia Cruz for treating me like a queen. And Faith Miranda for fueling the fire behind this book. A special thanks to my dear friend, William H. Caple III, for my video shoots, for building my website and a very cool logo. For listening to God about me and with me, thanks to you all.

To my girlz, Milinda Taylor and Lina Flannagan, thanks for doing what you do and always having my back.